Uncertain Health

Also by Stuart Friebert

Uncertain Health

poems by
Stuart Friebert

WOOLMER/BROTHERSON LTD
Andes, New York

Published by
WOOLMER/BROTHERSON LTD, ANDES, NEW YORK 13731
First Printing

The author and publisher are grateful for reprint rights to the following publications where many of these poems first appeared:

The Chowder Review: "Run Over Run Over"; *Cincinnati Poetry Review:* "What Can It Be, We're Not Dreamers"; *Contemporary Quarterly:* "Salmon," "More on Piers," and "The Metal Fox"; *CutBank:* "Three Hungarian Pieces" and "Every Year"; *Dark Horse:* "Brandy"; *Denver Quarterly:* "Old Joke" and "Fever"; *Epoch:* "Finnish Folktale" and "On Lying"; *Grain:* "Left Alone"; *Granite:* "The Crop" and "Hidden"; *Green House:* "Putting The Boat In"; *Huerfano:* "Milo" (Vol. 4, No. 2); *The Massachusetts Review:* "Has Been Recorded"; *Mikrokosmos:* "To Breathe" (©1977; reprinted by permission of the editors); *Moons & Lion Tailes:* "Very Well"; *the new renaissance:* "Whispering To The Guard" (Vol. III, No. 2); *Paris Review:* "Submarine Poem" (#64); *Pocket Pal:* "And" and "On Putting Your Daughter To Sleep"; *The Poetry Miscellany:* "You Two Go" and "Not As"; *Poetry Now:* "And Give Lessons To Your Son" and "Uncertain Health"; *Porch:* "On Teaching Your Father To Float"; *Quarterly Review of Literature:* "The Signal"; *Raccoon:* "For Women We Love"; *Seattle Review:* "Nothing To Say Now"; *Shenandoah:* "Dumb To Argue," "The Worst Yet," "More On Stealing," and "The Fall" (©1976, 1977 by Washington and Lee University, reprinted from *Shenandoah: The Washington and Lee University Review* with permission of the Editor); *Texas Quarterly:* "The Russian Window" (Vol. 18, No. 5; ©1975 by the University of Texas at Austin, and reprinted by permission); *West Branch:* "Your Father Dies Drowning." "The Apron" by Stuart Friebert was first published in *FIFTY CONTEMPORARY POETS: The Creative Process* edited by Alberta T. Turner. Copyright ©1977 by Longman, Inc. Reprinted by permission of Longman and the author.

"I wish to thank the Ohio Arts Council for a grant which was of great help during the writing of this book." — S. F.

Library of Congress Card Number: 78-68473
Cloth ISBN: 0-913506-08-7
Paper ISBN: 0-913506-09-5
Copyright © 1979 by Stuart Friebert
Printed and bound in the United States of America

for Dilly & Olly

CONTENTS

Parenting I

EVERY YEAR

Every year the fishing gets harder.
You want to doze in your father's arms.
Next best thing you go to the schoolyard,
sit on a swing, watch for falling stars.
A bat swoops low, that's that.

You hire a boat, go down river.
The moon hands over its crown.
All this time not a word.

Fish sitting together at one depth
and for half a minute you feel the glory
of not having schemed at all:

the hook you bait takes little thought.
A man hopes to catch his father a better fish.
Hints of spring in the water, wind pushing
hard to that bare little island every year.
He's fathering there.

YOUR FATHER DIES DROWNING

He tries to explain something, mutters dumb words.
Points to someone who can, goes back to sleep again.
You open his eyes, stand still, look at him perplexed.
Wait there against your will, his bones cheating him
of what they owe, knit again by night. Once he came
with three scars, a large one, a smaller one and one
tiny and bent, dust all over his boots, skin cracked.

If he ever does stop it'll be just when he passes his
schoolhouse again, the little swing stopped, sky the
color of hard silver. Speak to him, take everything
out again: the food, the wantonness and the avarice.
He'll whisper like your sister, steal upstairs, not
promise to stay. Anything like a struggle would have
been heard. Pull on the body, the best spot's stony
or sandy, free from wind, not deep. Willows and grass
at the sides, over which the water sometimes flows.

How could you have got him out of the water, his hair
the color he made his lures. The whitest, middle-size
minnows are best, you wish he were as long as an eel.
Pull his skin below the vent, let what drips be sauce.

ON TEACHING YOUR FATHER TO FLOAT

In the distance, between rows of trees,
a man's stamping his feet in the snow.
He seems to fall, gets up, falls down
again a different way, does this till
I reach him, see for the first time he's
my father, and I look down the way you'd
look down at a giant, slowly bending
your knees, leaning over while you do.
Getting him on your back at last, dream

you spend the whole night with him
on your shoulders, trying to keep your
balance. In the morning, the snow's
churned, a wonderful sea of fresh water!
You lay your father on the surface, his
head back, gently move his arms
till he moves them himself.

ACROSS THE LAKE

You turn your head slightly, no you can't
touch his hand. If only he'd look down, see
how you're doing, feet moving together well,
lungs pairing off, remember when you fell
down a lot? He yelled and didn't care much
who heard: inhale! The water tears your hair,
the boat's slipping sideways now, you have

a side view of temptation, come closer, so
there's no light or shade, is *that* him?

Quicker, the side of the boat before he sees,
just sheer alongside with a few good strokes,
collapse. No, that takes too much, better try
climbing in a moment, plenty of time left: exhale!

His hand trails the water, you're swimming harder,
part of what can be done never seems worth doing but
you're lucky, he's reminded of woods for a moment:
I'm going off to the woods, I mean I'll just get up

one morning and get the hell out of here, his voice
drags, his hands fill with oars. It's hard to hear
him now, if you keep stroking, his voice can only
lower or you could tread water, talk a while, level.

NOTHING TO SAY NOW

I'm going back, dad. That's all.
This country's yours, not mine.
I'll never learn how to hunt. I
just can't. He pretends to shoot
my gun, reloads, shoots it again.

It's the middle of the night, mom
begs to speak to me in another room.
Moon's pretty here, woods have plenty
of game, the water's good, why go back?

She steps outside to check the dogs.
I take her robe, wind it around her.
You better get up by four, I'll have
breakfast ready. She looks back at dad.

In the morning he wakes drowsy and slow.
If I'm not mistaken, he's gone, she says.
Since when have you ever been mistaken
about him? Dad gets his gun from the rack.

THE WORST YET

I come into the field where he's sitting.
He's set the lantern down, released the dog.
Dropped his gun. The moon's so solid it makes
his back itch. We ought to get on with it, dad.
You've been out here too long with nothing to show.
Your hand's trembling, see? Nobody will blame you.
I'll give them some sort of story when they find me
tied to the fence. Pick up your gun, start loading.

BRANDY

You stand in front of the barn,
take off your coat, put it
around your father. He sees
you have no shirt on, now he can't
look through you, can he? Wants
to live with you again, many men
from different towns are in the
same situation, they begin by
drinking brandy, climbing a hill
toward a cloud or two, they see
a son sleeping below. It's time
to wake him, they think, so they
roll back down. Each man measures
his body against the body of his son.

THE MEN

When they're all asleep, making wings
with feathers and wax, fitting them
to their bodies, the bodies of their
sons because there's much they can't
say, have after all spent evenings
in bedrooms, got up and gone to bathrooms,
waked up some more, shaved a little,
looked out windows, wanted to put on
coats and boots for a walk to friends'
but lingered over fears and kept them
for a moment. They seemed so abstract.

Even if all conditions are bad, hopeless,
they should go anyway. Even if other men
come from other houses, spend most of
their time there, when they do move they
scatter, it's a migration! And the path
they take is along some structure, say
the fence outside the window for instance.

WHAT CAN IT BE, WE'RE NOT DREAMERS

Kindle a fire, tell them to enter
the water when the moon approaches
the sun. Have all the men separate
from the women and both dive down
in different directions, nodding
their heavy heads, holding arms
before them as in a dark portrait.

Here's what they must do on crossing
the first layer of cold: immediately,
if only for a moment, have children.
Small hard ones that will be by them
till they reach the coldest water,
make slow and tiring movements, as if
fanning themselves with leafy branches.
The fatigue they feel will pass into
their children and be left behind.
They find that out when they pause,
touch each other's elbows. Finally,

on the bottom, which strikes them
as being very still, they put their
mouths to the stems and their voices
sound up from below, as if you held
a trumpet to your ear. If you hear
them, let them be, if the shock
of their descent will allow you to.

19

OLD JOKE

Without shame, quite openly, the old man
asks me to help him urinate. Why should he
have trouble in this warm weather? I think
of how much I could hate him, but there's
some pleasure in helping him open his fly
and pull it out. When the urine comes, I
look up, a bit surprised. Old man, I say,
I'll go shut the water off now and check
my tie in the mirror if you don't mind.
There's plenty of time to catch your plane.

He shakes his head, pulls his arm up his sleeve.
We got you when you was eight years old, he says.
The doc swore you was going to be all right, boy!
Then he pushes through the swinging door, taking
my mother with him. I sit down under the dryer
that keeps clicking off before I'm dry.

STAYING HOME

All right then, stay home, see if I care!
A huge, wire-hair terrier of a boy kneels
on the couch, looks out the big bay window.
The flag on the pole is still, the little
petunias in the bed at the base are pretty.
His father opens the car door, hangs a leg
out, Well, come on then! He motions hard,
Make up your mind! We want you along, I
take back what I said before. The boy shakes
his head again. Is that a Yes or a No, mother,
the man asks his wife beside him, I can't tell.

She's wearing a hat that looks like a catcher's mitt,
sipping beer, closing her eyes, putting the boy to
sleep in a far bed where there's less draft, calling,
softly at first: still the boy shakes his head No.
Sinks down out of sight, they wait five more minutes,
roll up the windows and walk back toward the house.

YOU TWO GO

Morning and your lips are very blue, you pull
on your boots, wake your father with a kiss,
gently lower your face to pat his, think
confession. Work his jaws up and down to
see teeth, cross from quarrel to subdue.
So your hands reach for the lid and
the baits are dull, the box green,
silence: stand mum, dad kidded.

Pet name for someone left behind, was younger
and wore more tweeds than anyone else's mother.
Kept the light out with pillar drapes, closing
them now and the light goes away. Her eyes open
again: You two go, go on now. Please. Just go.

Your father needs the company, son. Get along.
Oh you might send me a card when you get there,
but please, none of those junky, colored ones.
Lies down on her side, a move she made years ago.
Lying there, watching the shrubs twitch in the sun.

We began by renting a boat out of Boulder Junction,
a dirty boat filled with dried worms on the bottom.
Tipped it a bit when we jumped for the seat, came
as close as a wave here, there a wave, looked back:

Mother, Crooked Angel.

Dad gunned the motor, just missed the loon.
It squirted up on the other side, pushed
her five babies in five directions.

Dad whipped around and tried once more,
mother ran the water in the kitchen, had a sense
of humor for the card when it came: the two of us,
hunched over the side looking for a lost stringer.

When I tied it after the first bass it never caught.
Dad leaned way over, motioned with his whole arm.
I moved to the wrong spot, tried for him but fell.
You all right? Don't stand there in a boat like that,
okay? What would your mother think of my teaching?
Opens the beer, we drink her down in silhouette.

AND GIVE LESSONS TO YOUR SON

We start in the shallows, search for
the break, the drop-off. What kind of
bottom is that, dad? He doesn't seem
to care, he's watching an eagle fish,
it drops as if it's been shot, he says.
Pleased with the comparison. I try to
keep him talking, stories of the old
country, standing in cold mountain
streams with his father, moments spent
trying to swim if they heard shots and
the weeds didn't go over their heads.

Digging and digging and burning, burning
the bottoms of their feet, drying them
in the smoke of a fire if they could.
Terrible murders nearby, just when they
sat down to pray. And I see resemblance:
the way we eat with our hands, or order
the slave to destroy the child as soon
as it is born. It'll be a mud bottom,
dad looks down: Don't do as I did, fish
alone, take your time. Time. Why should
you hurry? And give lessons to your son.

PUTTING THE BOAT IN

Tired, swimming all night, breath has you by the throat,
what are you doing out in the middle? Feel your heart beat,
a lifeboat a child can't handle, would get his face wet, let
go your stroke, roll over: clouds, wind. Absolutely gone,
that's what you are, they could put the boat in, sick as
they are hanging around till you drown, shaking heads all
night, dry-talking. What are you supposed to do, swim for ice?

Your father tightens a nut, your mother turns a valve, then
they cut some pipe. Cloven hoof but cleft palate, she always
said, up the steps she went, that won't get the boat in, mom.

At this distance, you're nothing but a speck, keeps you from them.
They begin to doubt, go back to the boat when they can, smell it,
go over the whole surface, your father spits corks into the leaks.

Your mother brings cookies and milk on a tray. Another time he puts
a huge slab between two others, rings a little bell when he's done.
She checks her hair in the mirror before she comes, the last time

you see them she's holding a wrench, he's letting her watch. Moves it
across the wood, panics her with his mumbling. That's why it never
comes into her head to put the boat in alone. She sinks to the ground
by his side. If anything happened to him, they'd break the boat up.

LEFT ALONE

The boy adopts a new name to pass the time.
The parrot has trouble learning it and dies.
The mother yells from her mother's, Bury it
please before I get home, honey! So he takes
one wing, slides it down the garbage disposal,
instantly his mother yells from the slope
outside the window: Can Michael come out
and play? Christopher? Well Stephen then?

Her call's for a son a day's journey from
her delicious veal. He always had seconds.

But first she sent him off to the store
to return something she bought in a fit
of desperation. Something too big, something
she couldn't return herself. You buy anything
with the refund you want, honey. So he bought
two quarts of soda and when he came running
down the street she tossed him the ball.
To catch it he had to drop the bottles.

MORE ON STEALING

Your father's standing at one end
of the room, the light falling into
his book. He makes a mark, some kind
of old ceremony, one hand acting out
of deep gratitude, the other becoming
a stick that points in two directions:
back to all promises, ahead to thievery.
But nothing happens in the first half hour
after he catches you red-handed, dead to rights.
You eat a little, you behave, you put your arms up.

The second half hour he asks good questions:
the floor that breaks the glass, the curve
of the drawer, the little lock in the middle.
With a hairpin? Broken. Reaches down to push
the money hard against your hand, runs it
through your fingers, crosses bridges with it,
looks dazed all night. No argument, just heavy
breathing so the tent falls, don't ask for more,
he loves you less, lays a hand on your shoulder,
a dollar on the floor.

THE FALL

Run, mama! She doesn't, I swallow
her quickly, she makes me heavy,
I sway to the ground, roll over.

Dad picks me up, puts me in his cart,
agrees she's inside me. I flush and
he looks for water. There is none

so he does the next best thing, sits
on me in the hot sun, then we shake
hands and have a good visit. Then my

easy going madman of a father dumps me
down the hill. She tears free, it's late
when he finds her, together they start out

to look for me, I'm a small stone far below.
They scrape me up, skip me across the water.

Imagining II

FEVER

You turn your chair to the window,
practice the recorder, shadows start
moving but the light stays put, patches
of bright green winter wheat I mean.

Walking the fields this morning I rubbed
my hands, wanted to live. Even in terrible
weather there are funerals *and* weddings.

The next bed is taken. Singers turn to go,
I feel I've lost you without any desire to
get you back: spring comes, life changes.

Breaking a twig from one of the trees
you won't recognize me till I stop dead
in my tracks. Who stood here before,
happier than kings, tossing in fever,
who the hell anyhow?

ON LYING

As soon as I shut the window we were married.
She cried out, Max, isn't it terrible there's
so much lying in the world? The waves beat on
the rocks, millions of swans flew up, down to
the boat I followed her, she gave me an oar, kept
one for herself. Now look through these glasses
at the other shore, she said. And tell me why
you're going with me, Max. And Max, don't lie.

SALMON

It is not mentioned in the Bible.
Six pounds are considered a fair price
for a good wife, for any river in which
it's found, add a huge bridge overhead,
rocks and gravel, a town nearby, a black
stove where the cooking's done. Where
your son would think of looking if
you sent him on a hunt, but you've
never been that methodical:

the longest, most circuitous route
was chosen on the way across rough water,
it was dark in the net in fifteen minutes,
you resolved to keep a lookout for the moon,
nailed the fish to the boat, made the moon
and the fish flop together.

SUBMARINE POEM

I

You think of moving the captured submarine
to a permanent berth alongside the museum
in your city. A retired engineer who spent
years on a plan to move the Eiffel Tower
volunteers a practical suggestion, so you
stop traffic on a lovely night in summer
and, as thousands watch, you inch the sub
across the outer drive. When it's in place
you introduce a famous naval commander
whose dedication address is piped ashore.

II

At first, the interior of the sub
seems unbelievably complicated, a maze
of dials, valves and gauges, every
available foot of space occupied.
But listen to your guide, though you
lose a good deal of what she says and
she talks too much of how cramped
the quarters are, running her hand
over the checkered blue linen on the bunks,
and seems to idolize the enemy captain—
carefully she points to a picture of him
sitting on a horse on his farm in Bavaria—,
she will quit her job just before the tour
is over and press past you. Miss, stop!
Stop, Miss! everyone cries, plunged in grief.

III

The movies you see later in the museum theatre
are official navy films taken during the actual
battle. You press both hands on the slatted wooden
seat and stare up at the waves, they go higher and
your mind slides to the folding top on the washstand
which became the captain's desk when he lowered
the lid and drew the tiny blue curtain.

MILO

I put money in all Milo's pockets and still
he carries me off on his shoulder, everyone
in town talking of money, money saved, made,
lost, quarters slipping through the cracks in
the insulation, pennies streaming downstairs,
sounds heard the last time he carried me off.
But that was different, he even helped a boy
bent over a sewer, an old woman whose bills
blew across a cornfield, she blessed him and
he put me down. Now we can go back, he said.

There's a different hold on his mind now,
money is scattered all over the world, we're
immortal, nothing can kill our bodies, there's
no money left! Milo goes out past the heavy gate,
carrying me on his shoulder, his fist to his lip.
For a moment I fear he might turn to eating me.
See that tree, Milo? Just remember, when you grow
older and I'm gone, you'll try uprooting that tree.

Half cleft, it will reunite and trap your hands, wolves
will come and the money stay buried under that tree.

THE RUSSIAN WINDOW

You can tell from the light it lets in
it has the highest opinion of itself, enough
to waste, enough to see you standing there
balancing a gun muzzle on a glass of tea.
I'm jealous of that glass, it says. Don't
worry, you say, I'll spend the night. And
it seems relieved. But when you move over
to call from it, the window makes its move:

Don't do that, it's been a long day, I need
some sleep. See that blanket, tack it up over
me, I don't want half the things I see out there.
Help me show a flank of glass, I'm suffocating!

Need anything ironed for morning, I ask. Yes,
it mumbles, See that large shade over there? It's
no trouble, I whisper, slip down for the pantry
iron and the family handkerchief, start to work.

But I have a bad heart, bang into the table that
spills the tea that fires the gun that wakes it:
I suppose I can't keep you in the dark without
playing something. It starts playing trees, so
loud I want to cut its ropes and steal the weights,
but I strike the pane instead, like whistling
a snorer down. Firmly, three or five times, it
stops snoring now. The trees go away and so do I.

THREE HUNGARIAN PIECES

There's a hurdy-gurdy man on the block.
His *Csardas* starts slowly, moves faster
and faster, until your partner has been
whirled into a state. Birthdays, weddings,
funerals, christenings, national holidays
of one kind or another, there's always an
occasion for dancing and drinking, always
a Hungarian yelling: I drink when I'm dry,
I drink when I'm sad, glad, I always drink!

After graduating from elementary school you
enter high school on the advice of your Aunt
Mariska, you meet a boy whose father is
an authority, visit his home frequently. First
he tells you your people migrated from Spain
during the Great Inquisition, then he points
to your body: You're covered with millions of
fleabites, my boy. Change to clean underwear!

A boy vanishes, gruesome stories spread throughout
the country. Soldiers appear everywhere, everyone's
ordered off the streets. Years later, it's discovered
the boy ran off to Amsterdam to learn the trade of
diamond polisher, his jewels known the world over.
Now it's an accepted fact in Budapest that acquiring
them is more important than quarreling, underselling
your neighbor's produce. He brings it in from his farm
on a barge, or a dirty rowboat, or a flimsy sailboat.

NOT AS

At first, they buried their dead anywhere.
Usually where they were killed or died.
They turned their rakes over, stuck candles
on the spikes. One woman turned away, they
made her weigh the soil down with heavy stones
so the dead would stay in their graves, gliding
into this notion: Death in the village, Death as
"In This District," but not as Dead. Not as Done
Away With. Gone. Rather as Old. Old Man or Old Woman

they said and warned the children against entering
the fields, dressed in fur the fool led one little
boy through the snow. He taught him to throw balls
of ice at the trees, marked each with a glaze: a way
to return when they reached the last grave, knelt
down, too blind to count the tiny little stones.

STRAW

When their wine turned to vinegar,
crops blighted, iron rusted and bees
were driven from their hives, they
went mad, begged for straw from house
to house, wrapped an old woman with it
and put a match to her. Down the hill
she went, blazing. That's for all
your crimes, they shouted.

What? What've we done? they poked each other
the next morning. Blamed an old woman, huh?
And so they saw more clearly, went back
to the houses for more straw, this time
they built a straw man, dragged him through
town in a cart so all the people might see him.

When they set fire to him in the fields
the fire was so fierce they could make out
a man slipping out of the straw and running.
They were so stunned they threw their hands
to their eyes, turned to face the burning
figure: Old Woman, they cried, We're burning
the Old Woman, they clapped and cried.

UNCERTAIN HEALTH

The man went to the bathroom to look for blood,
not to smile respectfully at the mere pain in
his ass, he simply found it more interesting
to correct, in the gentlest manner, his body's
mistaken view of life. But when he stooped to
see his hole in the mirror, he was afraid. I'm
afraid this may be more than blood in my stool.

Recently they discovered a cyst the size of an onion
on my ovary, she wrote. In the exchange of letters
that followed, they both came to the word 'fragile.'
Life is Fragile, they agreed. You could even say
the light shone through them at this time, they
could be made to look foolish, you could spoil
their future if you were nothing but a surgeon.

But the man had an idea, he wrote to the woman
very early one morning: If we were nothing but
peasants, we could let our dog in, give him milk
and when he lapped the bowl clean we could take
a swig and say, May He Be Sick, May We Be Sound!
Help, what do you think, my Darling Kunigunde?

FOR WOMEN WE LOVE

We write their names slowly, each letter
right over the next, drive around the block,
never make the call: they're pediatricians
with very fat legs and perfect pitch, hard
to take to concerts, impossible to nourish.

We're of less use now than the worm whose
silk is spun, the silver maples have a year
at best, we fall to our knees before women
who are museum directors: Mary loves Frank,
that's what it says on the tiny card next to

the painting but on the painting you can't
even see it's Mary. There's an MA, possibly
an R, possibly a Y and down a bit something
like an F. The directors go back to their
offices upstairs, put the map of the museum

in our hands, we're on our own. We know it,
the guards know it. They slap us on the back
and over we go. Fear keeps us down, staring
up between their legs. We watch them eat at
night, some kind of liver paste, mornings we

add some weight, pull the lure deeper, start
on shore: soft as white moss and hard to see.
No lights so we come to the little bridge by
accident, the chill's so strong we think the
sun won't rise. But it always does, the water
parts, feeds itself smooth and the women stare.

THE CROP

It's likely to be your second time,
are wild, nearly everything you mean
changes meaning, sundown brings horses
and a woman trying to teach you how
to ride. She lowers part of her body
to pass the branch, looks back over
her shoulder. You raise the crop
but cannot strike the horse.

The horse expects you to! she yells.
But you can't, you just can't,
so you slip to the ground, walk
away, were going to walk away,
you think you walked away.

AND

Once by the young widow of the fire chief
who wanted to go on as soon as it was light.
Once I took hold of your bottle and, filling
a large glass, drank to the health of persons.

Once by the short order cook, sauteeing mushrooms
for herself, squeezed between the refrigerator and
the stove. Can I have some of those on my omelette?
You fretting for my mushrooms, honey? she would say.

And once by someone who kept standing when I waved
her to my seat. Please, Miss! Oh, that's good of you
but I couldn't, Sir. Then she pointed to the strap
she held on to and studied her bright orange transfer.

And once when you tried to run from me, I ran after you
to the woods, the woods! Leaves hardening, darkening.
And always we shall set out for the Next Day with our
children, who see and hear everything that passes by.

MORE ON PIERS

Claiming to have stacked it away for the winter,
you're satisfied. There's a book by your side, you
still believe in God, though He can see you're
worn out by indecision. Of course, in those days
the spirit of fate replied, people hugged their
mothers, dropped swords and before they reached
the end of the pier the fit had stopped. Right.

The pier's strict within the cove, receives anyone.
A child running down it, jumping, getting swallowed,
vanishing utterly. You testify you heard her calling.

In northern Wisconsin the best ones are green to hide
among the foliage. Wrong. Sometimes they're just grassy
mounds surrounded by shadowy trees. Wrong. By birches
that cast no shadow, moving vigorously back and forth.

HAS BEEN RECORDED

The best examples have to do with creation,
explanations of existence, the usual I suppose.
Stars maybe, the ant & the lazy cricket, a maiden
without hands, the beautiful & the ugly twin but not

the Jew among thorns. Not that. Except perhaps for
single syllables, the bird singing its last, shot at
over the wager, the Jew going into the thorns naked,
dancing in them and the doctors shaking with amazement,
letting the bird go and those thorns taking thousands

of years to spit up through the skin. We've used this story
to prove something, in comparison to all the other stories.

Marrying III

TO BREATHE

Into a skid we go, I've loved you
once in life, can't turn the rope
fast enough, nothing more is said.

You're upset, the straw's wearisome,
I kick it now and then. The moment
you take off your panties and bra

more children come, some die, I'm
ready, cup your hands, up you go!
Wanting to learn to ride bareback

each of us thought: Well, you're dead
but I'm alive, calmly got ready to
groom the horse, you pushed back its

heavy black hair, I sat down by its
legs, lifted each hard hoof, no sign
of you around the flank. Children are

born like this, we have nothing else
to do but watch the tail of the horse,
crouch a little, make foam come from

its mouth. A friend says it's like with
dogs, just breathe the air they breathe.
The same air, lay your nostril against

the horse's, inhale, exhale. Soon you're
exchanging the air in your lungs, your
eyes lifeless, huddling together with

muzzles joined, sinking to the bottom
of things that way. Where we first met.
Where we're to part. Or not have taken

care to keep a horse these twenty years.
By now the air's so warm it rises. Shake
your head, start breathing again, there.

Breathe your last. For we breathe wrong.
The horse breathes right, tiny and thin
and turns its head easily the other way.

PRESENCES

1

We're walking by a small lake. For observation, and practice.
We put our hats on a rock behind us, stumble from silence to
silence. Bears are said to kill fish with one swipe of their
paws, take a huge bite right out of the middle, their ears
changed by the gods. As delicately as possible you tell me
how you stayed downstairs till I fell asleep and you could
read in bed. Bed's not for reading, Carrie told Max, Max
told me. It's very beautiful here, you say, and face me.

2

Let's suppose you don't. Instead you shove your arms back as
fast as you can, I switch to a quick glance behind me too, so
everything would be sweet, if only we had held this pose.

3

We can't think of the right remark, fall over like logs, you
tell the story about the hunting dog with a stick in his jaws.
Means the whole field's filled with rabbits (so many you couldn't
shake a stick . . .). We see tracks in the snow, but who could
ever follow them now? I leave you alone, you leave me alone.

4

We've tried saying forceful things, put them on our shoulders.
Hunters feel it's still the place to come. After they clear
the table, usher the kids to bed, they stand out here quite
casually, their dogs by their side. Shhh, be quiet, you say.

RUN OVER RUN OVER

for Russell

It's not even your own flesh and blood.
Just a dog you run over on a country road.
You open the door slowly, walk back toward
the spot in the mirror. God, I've killed
something, just like that. What the hell
was I doing, not watching the road?

A gate slams, the farmer walking toward you
surprises the hell out of you. Before you can
say anything, he begs your pardon: That damn dog!

If you want to help bury him mister, there's a
spade over there, I'll get my kids. He picks up
the dog by the hind legs, swings it like a rabbit.

You stand there, maybe you're a little hard of
hearing, suppressing something: we all ought to
be related, have large families to look after.

You look over at the spade,
if you picked it up you'd throw it
clear out into the field.

THE APRON

The man's been pitying himself all Sunday long.
First he went down cellar to oil the generator,
see what the potatoes were doing. Then he took
a few baits from his tackle box, paint wearing,
hooks falling off. When he put the last fish of
the season back into the water it sank down to
the bottom, left a long streak of blood behind.
He dragged the boat to the car, in the mirror
the lake was greasy and thick. He put his foot
on the gas, it was like stepping on the woman's
apron, a pleasant apron with flowers and teacups
all over. The kettle was singing. And steaming.

When the man gets home there's nothing at the end
of the stringer in his hand, when the child runs
between the woman and man he makes strange sounds
they can't understand. When they put him to sleep
in a glass bed at night they look in from all sides.

VERY WELL

The moment you get back into bed, I get up. O
I used to slip a hand down your leg as far as
the little knot, tell you about a blizzard outside
I'd made up, could have gone on telling you, stopped
because you'd say something about a child down the hall,
up now, listening for any sound anything might make.
Revving the props of his models, snapping his shades.

Shhh, you said, setting your mind to sleep again, pulling
the spread around your head like an Arab. It's impossible
to be that silent, feel nothing, I thought; slipped pants
on and turned around in the door like a bad actor before I
shut it clean. In the kitchen, over brandy, I made a sketch
of this house, spent the most time getting the swing of doors
just right. A little twist of compass, a little dash of hinge.

ON AGREEING

for Diane

We agreed about the pigeons. They should be shot
by the kid next door for a dollar a bird. He'd take
the shovel and gun from my hand, bury them out back
till he couldn't stand it anymore. A highschool hero
crying and why not, we felt bad too. Agreed about
the bat, the police would have to come, you kept it
in sight while I ran for the net. The bat broke low,
flew right over the rug, you thought you were safe
under the pingpong table! What a scream you've got.

Want it saved or wasted, mister? the cop said. Saved,
I whispered, followed her out to the bushes, couldn't
believe it headed straight for the chimney again! Can
I give you more inventory, Love: Remember we slid in
all the way from the turnpike that night, drove round
and round the streets, what white houses this town had
or was it just the snow? Want that house? I'll get it
for you, the real estate guy said. Didn't he know it
belonged to the mayor? Rang the bell, shook his fist,
we had sense to run before the door opened. What do you
make of these little chills, what if they reach the heart?

THE SIGNAL

The wife is writing something about betrayals.
When the husband goes through her room her head
turns slightly: Good Day! She is schön, her hair
like an icon's, she mumbles something about having
to hurry to church. In the distance, we can see her
holding a bouquet of misty yellow dandelions
out to a priest. He says Oh thank you,
she says Thank you, too.

It isn't the words, it's the darkness and the priest
kisses her in front of the broken window. Another
betrayal forms magically in her kidneys. This
woman, is she nothing to us? Her husband
enters another house before she returns
and can't be extracted.

I only want one thing, he says. There should be
no mistake please: I've seen red borscht in my dreams
for years now, and kind, unintelligent Jews on sacks
in the street, waiting for roofs to fall, for women
to signal the secret police who pretend to be porters
in front of the hotel across the dirty street.
They are a sight for sore eyes!

The husband rushes the picture to a developer
who makes enlargements. He looks dumb as he descends
the steps of his apartment. How is the wife getting on?
Thoughts of her mingle with his voice.

The police rush past shouting Passover!
Later she remembers him; she will say,
How is my Jew, my Elijah,
my little handful of scorched earth?

DUMB TO ARGUE

(Guess I'll turn in). You stand up,
stretch, run the vacuum over the rug
one more time, then you face her. No
pew, just knees. She's wearing her
puzzle on the couch, you pick up
her pencil, toss it back (Do you
know the only official Egyptian
religion in the fifteenth century?).

There's no hotel in town (Thanks,
thanks). (Do you want me to put the
cat out, run the bulb under the hood
so the car will start, sweetheart?).
It's winter no matter what we do.
(Thanks, thanks). Less than two words
from her, ask her what she has for
the wash (Just my slip and bra, oh
put these socks in too, who'll get
up with the kids, can you? Turn on
the blanket, I'll be up soon).

The weight of the steps under your
feet is some mistake, you stare back
down through the hall into the den,
Chinese checkers stick out from
under the couch! Who said anything
about a game at this hour? (Goodnight!).

(Anyhow, goodnight honey). (I said
goodnight). She doesn't look up and

by and by your hand slides up the
banister, you can go the short way
alone, weigh yourself on the old
scale, put the blanket on, slide
your cramped legs down to the end
of the sheets. Speech against the
rich, one against the poor, sleep.

You get up early, cover the kids,
make some sandwiches and slip your
hipboots on. Near the dam you cast
out, the fly rises in the mist before
it loops over, the water is full of
little suitcases, floating off.
You lean way over, just miss
the handle of one, go into
hysterics:

it gets darker, you take your boots off,
shake the water out, it gets lighter.
And a new word is created to take
your place, pronounced, you're
totally lost and not revived,
never going to be.
No you're not.

HIDDEN

A little way back from the water-soaked clothes,
believing the funny thing, that the cocoon slips
out of the tree and is brought to the father by
the daughter who has enough evidence to hang him.

He looks her way after she turns the burners off,
makes sure she's set the table, poured the milk.
To protect it from the birds, rain or snow feed it
the leaves of the very tree it fell from, he says.

The way she looks at him when he hurries his food.
The simple shape of the diamond dessert!

ON PUTTING YOUR DAUGHTER TO SLEEP

Gets so quiet she sticks her head through
the slats, someone coming out, showing you
a wedding cake, piece chipped off the tree,
minnow on top of water. Dizzy with pain.

Grab an oar, see as much water as you can,
rub her temples. She goes on singing to her-
self, holds on with one hand and the sorrows
multiply. Tell her lie back down please, turn

out the light, she points. Smells of cypress.
She fights off sleep some more, you sweep all
her animals up, prop them against the wall, now
she tears her mouth to a grin and one night sleeps.

THE METAL FOX

You sink the metal fox into the ground.
Years go by, you forget where it stands.
Don't dream it will cut his leg when he
goes into the brush to hide from you, it
was winter, who could miss it, branches
were bare. It was serious, shots needed.

And the florist decorated the room with
masses of scarlet yellow flowers, you're
the only ones on the corridor that night.
The room dim, the snow stopped. Someone
in a coma like that's your son, you want
baying hounds, hunting horns, anything
to make life huge, go right up to it.

No idea where to go, running off
like that, fleeing a father's anger,
drawing out of brush the metal fox
no one was looking for.

AND ANOTHER

Before I sharpen the knife
I take a look over at the eye,
it tilts if the tail slaps the plate,
tilts or rises, would rise all night
in an empty kitchen, throw away memory.
I press it back down with a thumb,
it's about the end of the 20th century,
fish in the lake nearby are scarce, I
should scale them before I leave for home
the old fisherman says, so the slime won't
freeze. But the markings go, old man,
Don't you know that? You know, I think
I just touched a tongue, right there,
that soft gray petal, must be a tongue,
hey kids come here!

When they come running to the sink I put a hand up:
We won't be eating this fish tonight, it's not enough.
Sorry, it's not! (Dad, that's what you always say . . .).
That's enough or I'll lose my temper, enough now!

I know they're frightened, keep adding up the ones
I've caught since we bought the boat. Still, on such
a day there the fish was, all by itself, down by that
stump. Then it splashed and all I did was pick up anchor,
row over, give it my smallest minnow. When I cut in,
the kids giggle. The fish seems to fart a little.

I wash it off, hurry it into the plastic bag and,
having frozen it, blow on my hands, hug the kids.
The only thing can still their hunger is another
fish, and another.

WHISPERING TO THE GUARD

My children will sleep nearer
the door this year, May, June,
what difference does it make,
I take my shirt off, there are
more in the drawer, come down
stairs with a heavy list, pour
more scotch, drink more slowly,
try to understand: they're off,
floating off, goddammit. The ice
is broken, just kneel down and
give the pieces a little shove.
Put some teeth into it, smash
the cradle, throw it back to
the tree, when did I plant that?

Did you have a good day in school?
They fold their hands up in mine,
shoulders lining the dark, an old
vase sails past the moon. George
the barber leans over their heads,
banks the mirror. Yes, that's fine
George, just fine. Their mother will
be pleased. Here, pay the man, kids.

I open my eyes. The painting I want
is over the mantle, there's an old
man gazing at it, whispering to the
guard. Between two blue ash snow
getting darker and the little bed
in the corner burning till morning.